HOW TO DRAW ANIMALS
FOR THE ARTISTICALLY ANXIOUS

FAYE MOORHOUSE

HARPER

ILLUSTRATED BY FAYE MOORHOUSE
EDITED BY LUCIENNE O'MARA, SOPHIE SCHREY AND PHILIPPA WINGATE
DESIGNED BY ZOE BRADLEY

First published in Great Britain in 2017 by LOM ART, an imprint of Michael O'Mara Books Limited,
9 Lion Yard, Tremadoc Road, London SW4 7NQ www.mombooks.com

HOW TO DRAW ANIMALS FOR THE ARTISTICALLY ANXIOUS

Published in 2018 by
Harper Design
An Imprint of HarperCollins*Publishers*
195 Broadway
New York, NY 10007
Tel: (212) 207-7000
Fax: (855) 746-6023
harperdesign@harpercollins.com
www.hc.com

Distributed throughout North America by
HarperCollins Publishers
195 Broadway
New York, NY 10007

ISBN 978-0-06-269150-7
Library of Congress Control Number 2017935991

Printed in Malaysia

Second Printing, 2023

INTRODUCTION

Does the sight of paper, pens, and paints make you panic?
Can the fear of creating a less-than-polished piece of art make you anxious?
Fear no more. A rescue remedy awaits.

This book is a safe space for you to let loose your inner artist, without
the pressures of precision and perfection. Eradicate your eraser—shaky
lines, scribbles, and splotches are all welcome. They are applauded.
Hooray for weird and wonky art!

Transform a multitude of painty splotches into animals, from meerkats
to mice. Each spread features a different animal, with a watercolor
shape and suggested features for you to copy or take inspiration from.
Allow Faye Moorhouse's illustrations to guide you, help you, and
celebrate quirkiness in all its glory.

You are as unique as the animals in this book.
What are you waiting for?
LET'S DO THIS!

FLAMINGO

Dreaming
about fish

YAY! Caught
a fish

He stole
my fish!

Gutted

Normal legs

Sleeping
legs

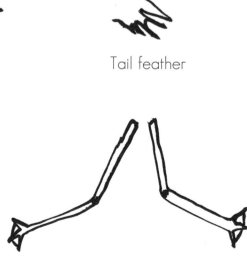

Tail feather

Had-one-too-many-
cocktails legs

PENGUIN

Sad face

Striped sweater

Bow tie

Necklace

Smelled-a-bad-fish face

Angry face

Egg

Happy feet

Too much mascara

Feet

Shy feet

BUTTERFLY

Everyday wings

Party wings

Eyes

Antennae

Body

A light lunch

BEAR

Salmon for supper

HUGE salmon
for supper

Enforced diet

Legs

Ears

Arms

RACCOON

Masked
avenger

Burglar

Ears

Tail stripes

Arms

Striped burglar shirt

Swag bag

Legs

DOG

Need to be pet

I ♡ being pet

OK. Too much petting

Eyes

Happy tail

Sad tail

Collars

Front legs

Back legs

TORTOISE

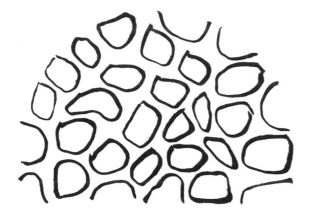

Simple shell

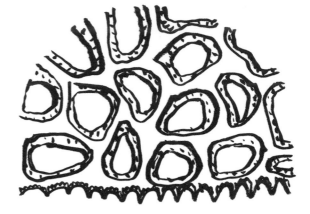

Fancy shell

Dancing feet

Tired tortoise

Happy tortoise

Attack tortoise

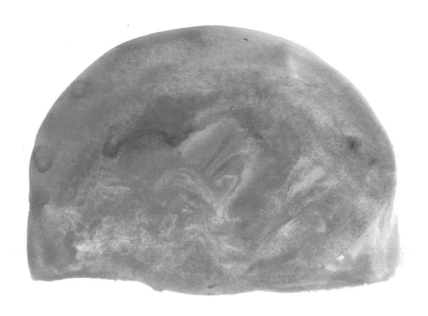

PANDA

Snoozing

Snacking

Sulking

Smug

Ears

Arms

Legs

Bamboo

CAMEL

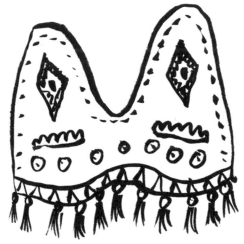

A magic carpet

Amorous smile

Kiss me, quick!

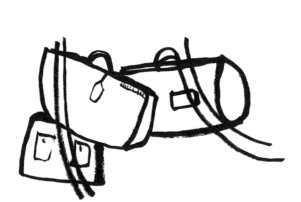

Lots of luggage

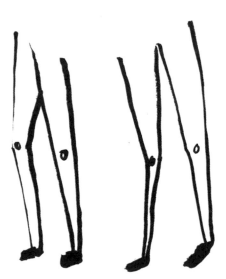

Legs

Tail

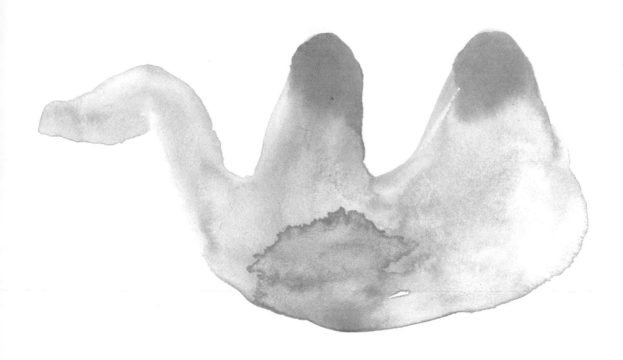

PiG

Possessed

Surprised

Down in the dumps

Spots

Happy tail

Hair

Sad tail

Legs

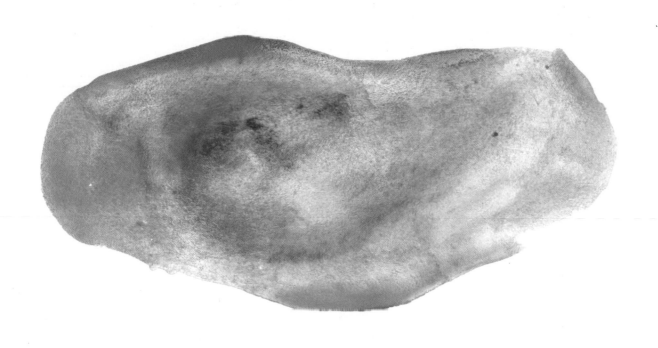

 # MEERKATS

Daydreamer

Mischievous

Anger issues

Bored now

Whiskers

Fur

Just chillin'

DANGER!

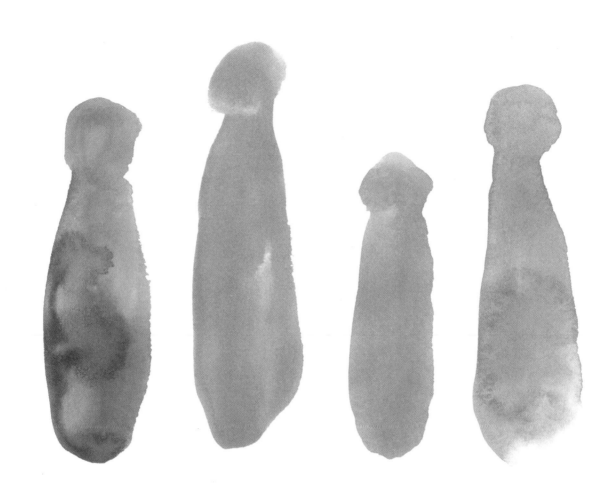

SQUiRREL

Hungry
face

Confused
face

Shocked
face

Fierce face

Sad face

Whiskers

Legs

Arms

Ears

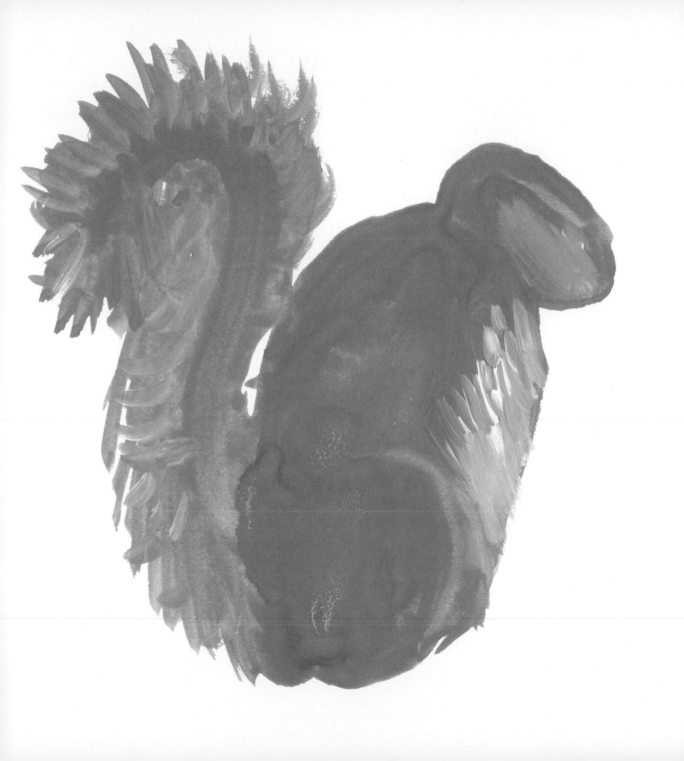

BEE

Simple wings

Antennae

Eyes

Striped wings

Stinger
(don't touch!)

Six legs

Fancy wings

SHEEP

Perm

Ate too much grass

Don't mess

Mischievous

Sheepdog alert!

Legs

Big ears

Small ears

PEACOCK

Snooty

Vexed

Troublemaker

Buzzing

Fabulous feathers

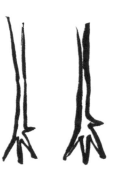

Legs

Crest

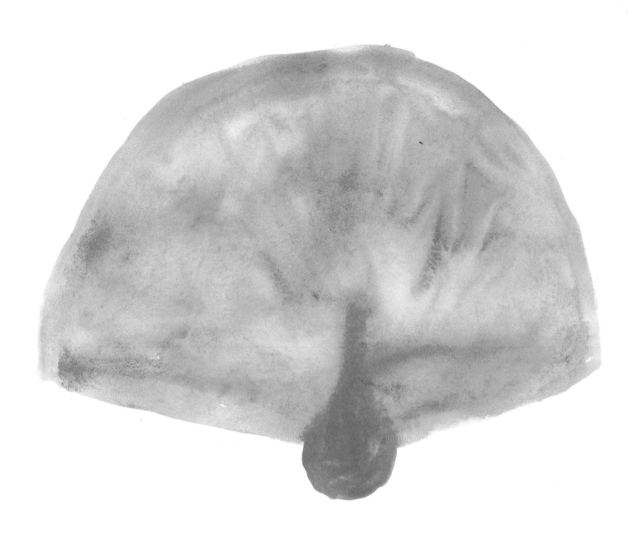

SHETLAND PONY

Groomed mane

Sleep deprived Friendly

Messy mane

Short legs Tail Ears

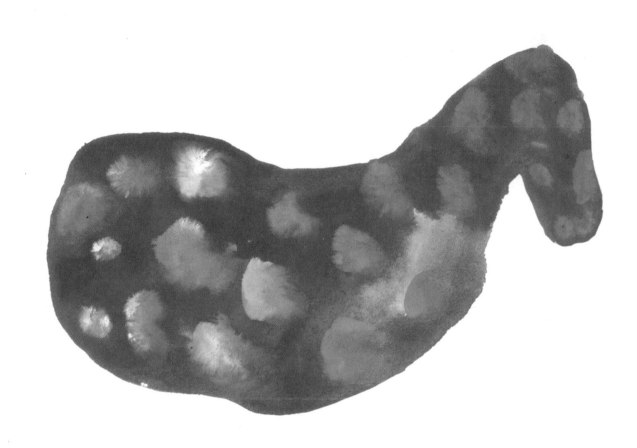

CAT

Tortoiseshell

Eyes

Front legs

Tabby

Back legs

Bengal

Which tail shall
I wear today?

Devotion

Disdain

MONKEY

Grumpy
face

Happy
face

Sneezy
face

Sleepy
face

Shy
face

Startled
face

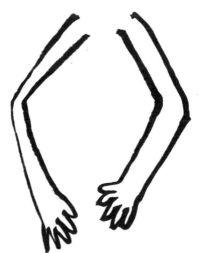

Arms

Legs

Ears

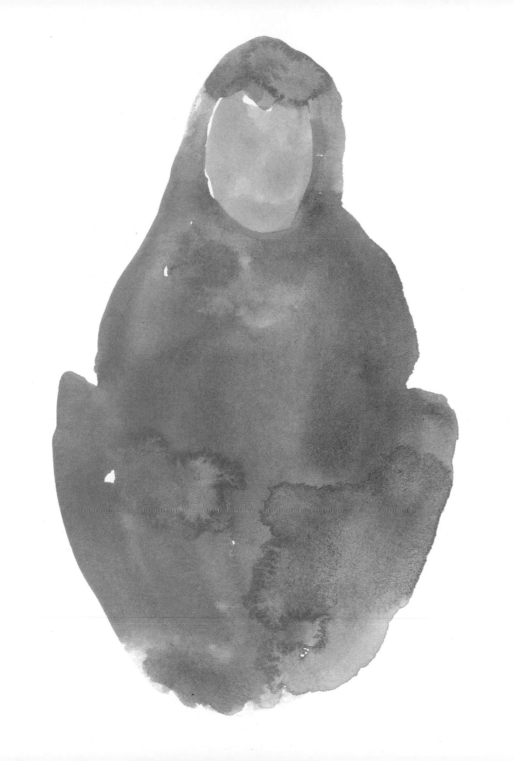

GUiNEA PiG

Surprised face

Windswept hair

Lettuce face

Lunch

Blow-dry

Ears

Feet

RABBIT

Tall ears

Short ears

Floppy ears

Handlebar ears

Fluffy
tail

Eyes

Nose and
mouth

Curious whiskers

Front paws

Back paws

Curly fur

Bad fur day

FROG

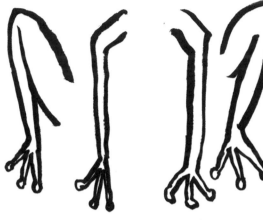

Legs

Happy

YUM. A fly!

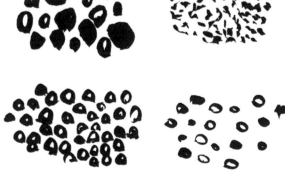

Cute camouflage

Actually, I think it was a bee

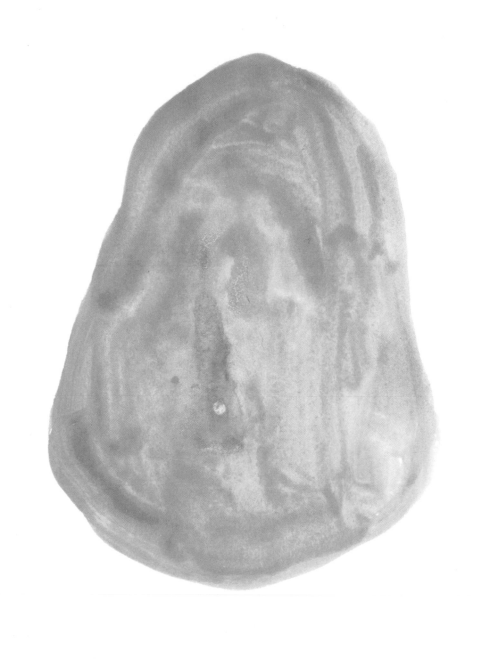

GiRAFFE

Alert eye

Flirt eye

Mouth

Mmm... leaves

Mane

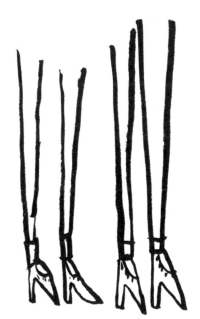

Horns

Long legs, high heels

Tail

Ears

Patches

COW

Why the long face?

Horns

Back legs

Front legs

Ears

Tail

I'm over here

Splotches

Udder

SHARK

Happy shark

Fish-eating shark

Hammerhead shark

Gills

Baby fin

Adult fin

Great white fin

Belly fins

WALRUS

Not impressed

Needs a shave

Shaving rash

Front flippers

Tail

Extreme-aging wrinkles

CHICKEN

Beady eye

Feet

Small beak

Simple crest

Wing

Medium beak

Jazzy crest

Tail feathers

Large beak

Bad hair day

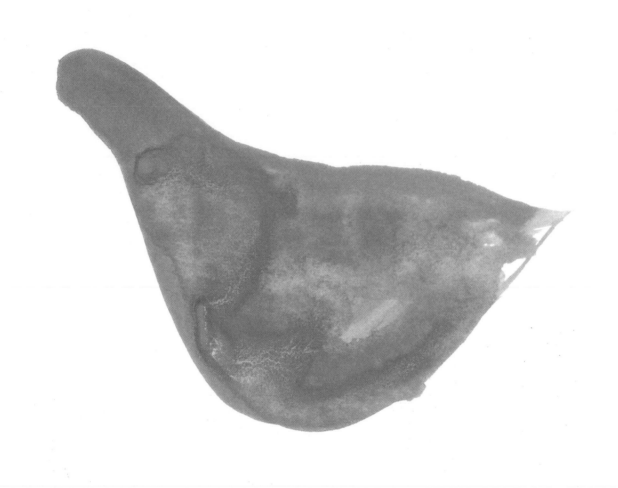

LEOPARD

Actually, you *can* change
a leopard's spots

Tail

Ears

Whiskers

Legs

Glum face

Game face

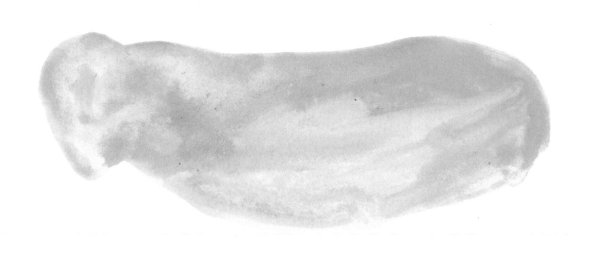

KOALA

Fluffy ears

YUM!

Super chilled

Spiky ears

Eucalyptus branch

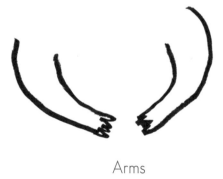

Arms

Ear muffs

Legs

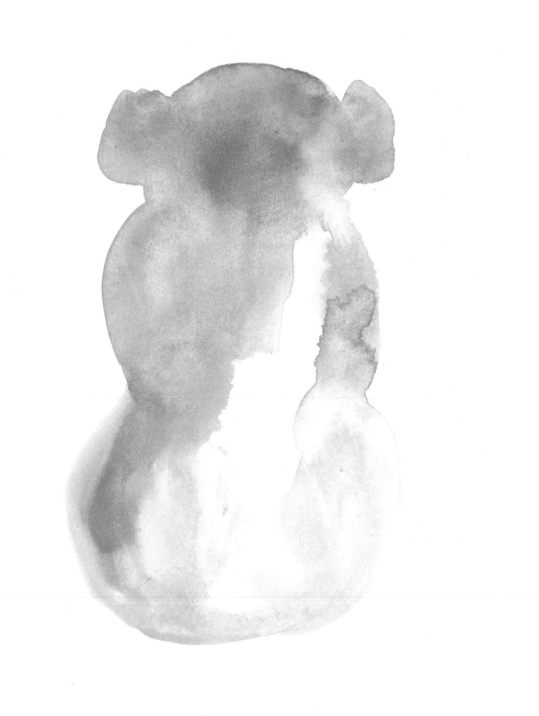

SPiDER

Neat
spider's web

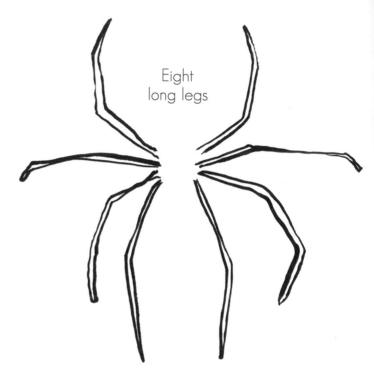

Eight
long legs

Messy
spider's web

Hair

Eyes

POODLE

Fancy bouffant

Simple, understated
curls

Eyes

Pom-pom tail

Feeling
coy

Feeling
good

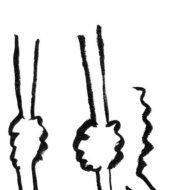

Fluffy ears

Legs

Curls

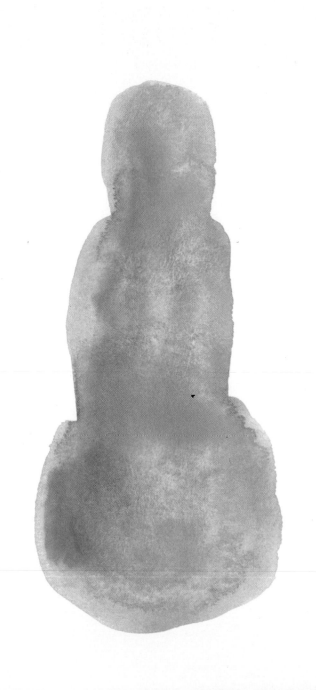

OSTRICH

Are you looking at my egg?

Do NOT take my egg

STEP AWAY FROM THE EGG!

Egg

Legs

Tail feathers

Hair

Body feathers

 # DEER

Small antlers

Boss antlers

Christmas antlers

Eyes

Ears

Nose and mouth

Tail

Legs

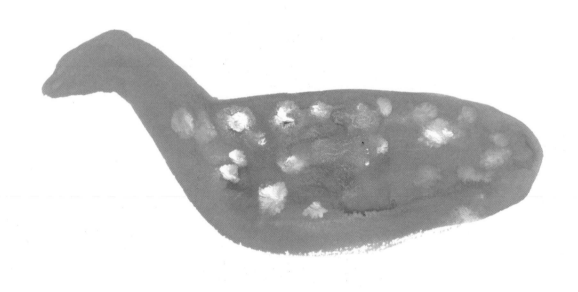

ZEBRA

Dainty ears

Eyes

Stripes

Nose and
mouth

Hairy ears

Messy mane

Legs

Tail

Punk piercing

Styled mane

SNAKE

Look into my eyes

Back off

Ouch, I bit my tongue

Shake your rattle

Crosshatch pattern

Polka dot

Scaly skin

ELEPHANT

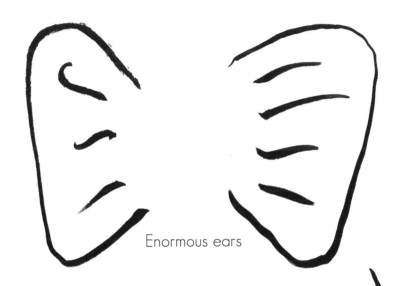

Enormous ears

Curly tusks

Tiny tusks

Eyes

Nostrils

Toes

Tail

Bollywood tusks

 # TiGER

Stripes

GRRRR!

Indifferent

Surprised

Sad

Pick 'n' mix eyes

Whiskers

Back legs

Front legs

Ears

Tail

WHALE

Grooves

Front fin

Whale tail

We're with the whale

Angry face

Sad face

Happy face

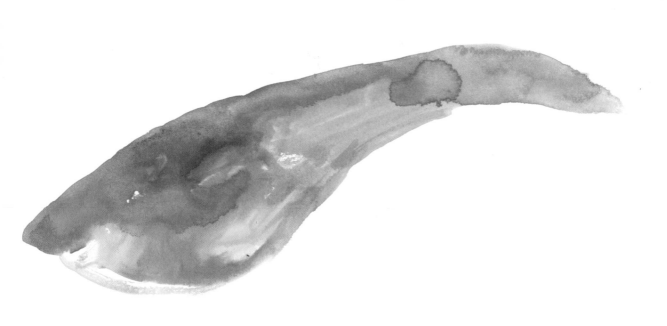

HORSE

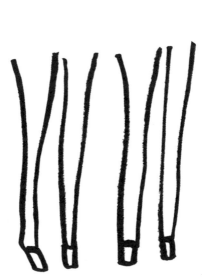

Braided mane

Short mane

Mane in bows

Flowing mane

Angry face

Pretty face

Tail

Clip-clop

Ears

Stuffing my face

Burp!

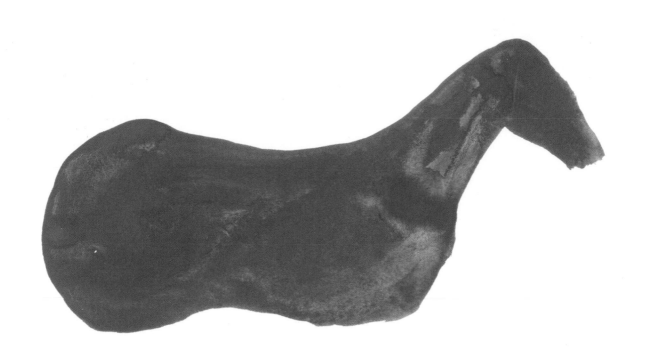

MOUSE

Ears

Eyes

Greedy paws

Back legs

Tail

Tiny paws

Nose and mouth

Cheese!

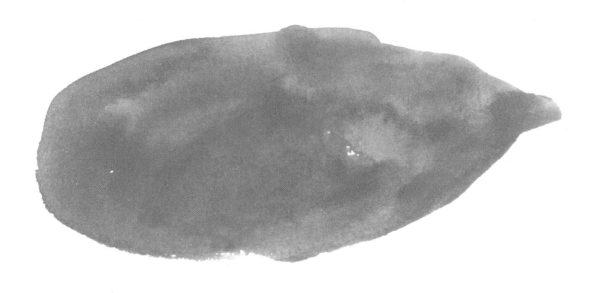

LiON

Eyes

Tail

Back legs

Front legs

Pick 'n' mix noses and mouths

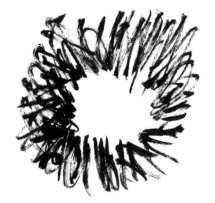

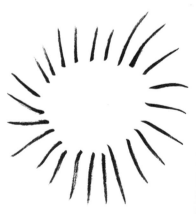

Groomed mane

Bad hair day

ELECTROCUTED!

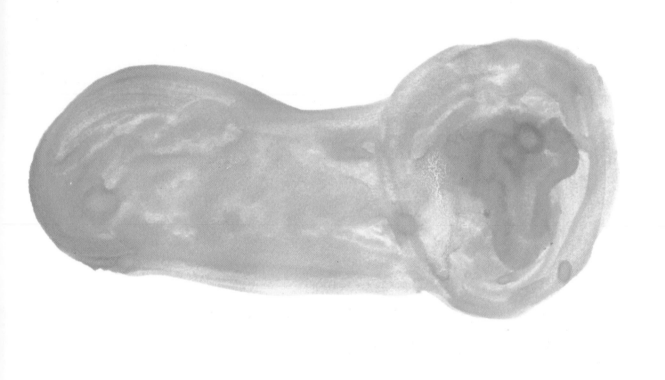

OCTOPUS

Big eyes

Wrinkles

Shifty eyes

Suckers

Tentacles

HEDGEHOG

Soft spikes

Spiky spikes

Fauxhawk

Smug

Thoughtful

Leaves

Ears

Legs

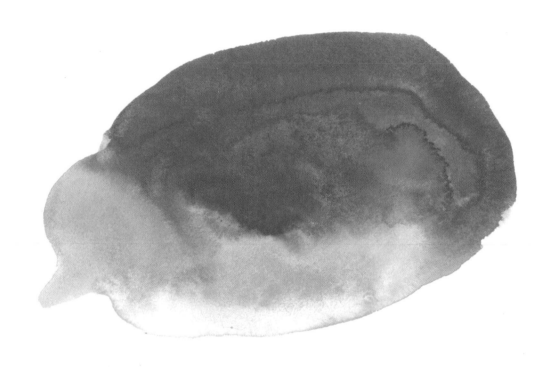

RHiNO

Are you looking
at me?

Big horns

Happy tail

Sad tail

Nose

Tiny horns

Regular legs

Mouth

Wrinkles

These-stockings-are-too-big legs

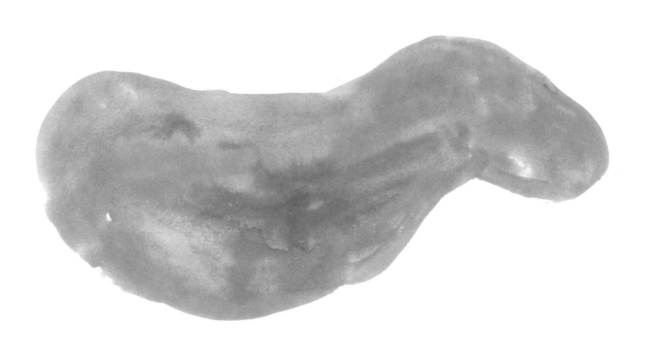

TOUCAN

Svelte body

Wing

Shocked eye

Wizard hat

Cowboy hat

Feet

Evil eye

Bowler hat

FiSH

Fins

Plain tail

Flashy tail

Mouth

Enormous eye

Scales

Party eye

SNAiL

Simple shell

Pretty shell

Disco shell

Angry

Sad

Surprised

Feelers

Full-body tattoo

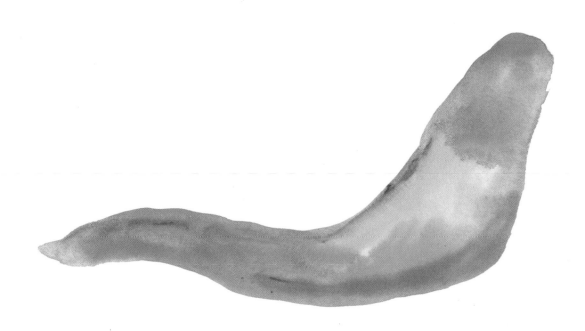